SYSTEMATIC / SUBJECTIVE
COLOUR SELECTION

An AVA Book
Published by AVA Publishing SA
c/o Fidinter SA
Ch. de la Joliette 2
Case postale 96
1000 Lausanne 6
Switzerland
Tel: +41 786 005 109
Email: enquiries@avabooks.ch

Distributed by Thames and Hudson
(ex-North America)
181a High Holborn
London WC1V 7QX
United Kingdom
Tel: +44 20 7845 5000
Fax: +44 20 7845 5055
Email: sales@thameshudson.co.uk
www.thamesandhudson.com

Distributed by Sterling Publishing Co., Inc.
in the USA
387 Park Avenue South
New York, NY 10016-8810
Tel: +1 212 532 7160
Fax: +1 212 213 2495
www.sterlingpub.com

in Canada
Sterling Publishing
c/o Canadian Manda Group
One Atlantic Avenue, Suite 105
Toronto, Ontario M6K 3E7

English Language Support Office
AVA Publishing (UK) Ltd.
Tel: +44 1903 204 455
Email: enquiries@avabooks.co.uk

ISBN 2-88479-057-8

10 9 8 7 6 5 4 3 2 1

Written and designed by
Andrew Bellamy
Typeset in Trade Gothic and Univers

Production and separations by AVA
Book Production Pte. Ltd., Singapore
Tel: +65 6334 8173
Fax: +65 6334 0752
Email: production@avabooks.com.sg

SYSTEMATIC / SUBJECTIVE
COLOUR SELECTION

Andrew Bellamy

HOW TO USE YOUR COLOUR SELECTION AID

The front and back of this card show the position and classification of colours on the colour wheel and provide the precise percentage values that allow the perfect mixture of colours when designing in CMYK mode.

These are the percentage values of Cyan, Magenta and Yellow that can be typed into the colour-mixing panel of a design program to create perfect primary, secondary and tertiary colours. The border indicates the colour that the percentage values produce.

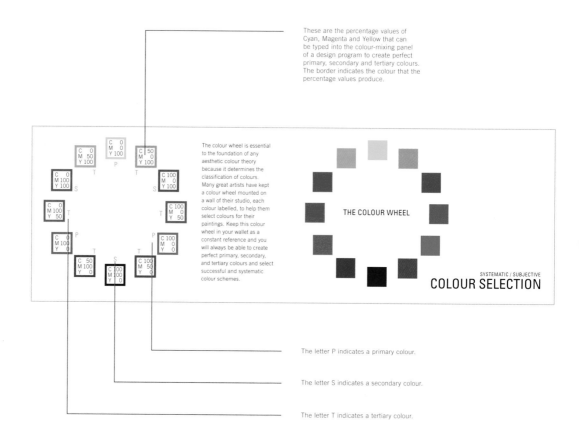

The colour wheel is essential to the foundation of any aesthetic colour theory because it determines the classification of colours. Many great artists have kept a colour wheel mounted on a wall of their studio, each colour labelled, to help them select colours for their paintings. Keep this colour wheel in your wallet as a constant reference and you will always be able to create perfect primary, secondary, and tertiary colours and select successful and systematic colour schemes.

THE COLOUR WHEEL

SYSTEMATIC / SUBJECTIVE
COLOUR SELECTION

The letter P indicates a primary colour.

The letter S indicates a secondary colour.

The letter T indicates a tertiary colour.

The inside of the card provides quick reminders of the
systematic colour selections detailed in the book. The solid
black squares on each wheel illustrate a different systematic
colour selection / scheme and represent selected colours.
These squares can be rotated in their groups around the
wheel to create a number of combinations.

For example, this diagram illustrates
that a complementary scheme is
made from two colours directly
opposite each other. It does not imply
that a complementary scheme can
only be made from the colours at the
very top and bottom of the wheel as
the black marks can be moved around
to select any two colours, as long as
they remain directly opposing.

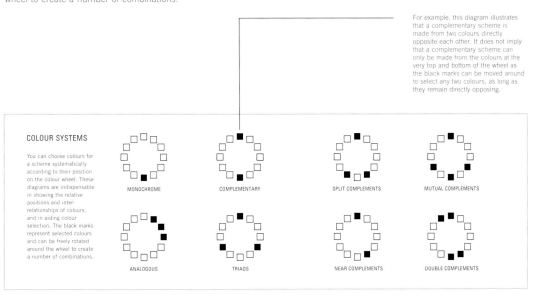

COLOUR SYSTEMS

You can choose colours for
a scheme systematically
according to their position
on the colour wheel. These
diagrams are indispensable
in showing the relative
positions and inter-
relationships of colours,
and in aiding colour
selection. The black marks
represent selected colours
and can be freely rotated
around the wheel to create
a number of combinations.

MONOCHROME   COMPLEMENTARY   SPLIT COMPLEMENTS   MUTUAL COMPLEMENTS

ANALOGOUS   TRIADS   NEAR COMPLEMENTS   DOUBLE COMPLEMENTS

CONTENTS

INTRODUCTION

There are many factors and areas of theory that can be taken into consideration when selecting colours for a design. These areas can be used to evoke a desired emotional or personal response from the viewer. However, the success and effect of these choices is limited by the individual viewer's comprehension and appreciation of them depending on background, experience and taste.

Colour can be used to evoke psychological emotions, whether excited subconsciously or through a learned association. For example, a dominantly red design may make us feel warmth or suggest aggression, or equally the instruction to stop. Although such associations can provide a powerful design tool it is important to realise the result is limited and culture specific. In different cultures colours may carry different meanings and an emotive response will not be universally understood. Just as the success of certain colour schemes

may not travel across physical geographic boundaries, others may not survive the boundaries of time. Fashion often plays a powerful role in leading designers to make specific colour selections. However, it is important to realise that any colour selections made according to the commercial vogue will, as with all trends, prove popular for only a brief period. The success and appeal of these choices is ephemeral.

Any colour selection made according to what's popular at any one time is done so at the expense of the reflection of subject or personality of the designer. Personal choices made according to one's own taste and preference can reveal a great deal about the designer and can add a signature to a series of works. However, the resulting designs may only be attractive to those related in preference, alienating a potentially larger audience.

There are clearly problems with any personally or locally
inspired colour scheme and the only way to produce designs
that please a wide audience is to produce designs that please
the eye, not the mind. This section of the book contains
systematic colour selections that please the eye through their
relationships with each other. The colour schemes may not
be acceptable across cultures, fashions, or evoke emotion,
but they provide a basis for harmonious balance in design
that is universally pleasing and accepted. Prior to the
discussion of any colour selection the basic principles
of colour such as its different forms and dimensions are
discussed. An understanding of these objective principles
is essential to the correct evaluation and successful use of
colour in design. This knowledge will provide the foundation
on which successful use of colour can be built.

PRINCIPLES

ADDITIVE AND SUBTRACTIVE COLOUR

Graphic designers are constantly involved with two forms of colour mixing; additive and subtractive. It is important that the differences between the two are understood before any mixing or selection of colour is undertaken.

Additive Colour

Colours made by light are referred to as additive due to the fact that as more colours are added to a mix the lighter the mix becomes. In the past this has only really been of concern to the physicist and the designer has not been required to understand the principles of coloured light. However, the advent of computer graphics introduced the designer to additive colour as it is the principles of coloured light that allow the everyday, immediate, precise, and clean production of colour on our computer screens. Cathode ray tubes used in computer monitors have three electron guns corresponding to the primary colours of light; red, green, and blue (RGB). When these three hues are mixed in equal proportion the result is white light (1). When the beams from these three guns strike a light-sensitive coating on the screen in varying combinations and intensities, they can create an array of luminous colour sensations. Computer monitors can produce a large gamut of colours, almost 70 per cent of what the human eye can differentiate.

Subtractive Colour

Subtractive colour is the term associated with physical colour such as paint or objects. Colours seen on the surface of physical objects, such as paper, work in very different ways to those seen in light. When light strikes a surface certain wavelengths may be absorbed and others reflected by colouring matter; pigments. The reflected wavelengths blend to form the colour seen by the viewer. For example, a blue object absorbs all wavelengths except blue which is reflected back into our eye, resulting in the perception of blue. An object that appears black absorbs all wavelengths and an object that appears white reflects all wavelengths. Established artistic theory recognises three pigment colours – blue, red and yellow – to be primary colours that cannot be mixed from other colours but from which all other colours can be mixed. However, the ability to physically mix all other colours is only possible with printer's inks: cyan, magenta, and yellow. Unlike colours mixed in light, as more subtractive hues are mixed, the mix becomes darker; the mixture of pigment subtracts light (2).

In theory, when the three primary hues are mixed in equal proportion the result will be black, but it is in fact a very dark brown. Black is therefore added as a fourth printing ink to create darker areas. These three hues together with the white of the paper and addition of black to deepen dark areas can be used to produce many colours. The gamut of this four-colour printing process (CMYK) is only 20 per cent of what the human eye can distinguish, much less than that of the computer monitor.

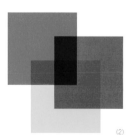

(1)

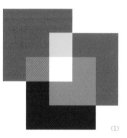

(2)

COLOUR MODES

One of the most versatile parts of modern design software
packages is the way that they work with colour. Covering
design that will be used on screen and design that will
be output for print they contain various colour modes.
These are determined by the eventual delivery of design.

For Web or multimedia, colours should be selected in the
RGB (red, green, blue) colour mode, and mixed with the
RGB colour palette. The RGB colours are used by computer
monitors to display full-colour work on screen. They offer a
very wide colour range, allowing the choice of colours at a
very high saturation.

For printed work design must be executed in the CMYK
(cyan, magenta, yellow, key / black) colour mode and mixed
in the CMYK palette (see opposite). These are the colours
used by most desktop printers and digital/offset printers to
reproduce full-colour photographs and illustrations. Colours
mixed in this mode should therefore reproduce well in print.

DISCREPANCY BETWEEN SCREEN AND PRINT

It is important to be aware that when designing in CMYK mode we work on an RGB monitor that uses additive technology to simulate the results of subtractive colour. Consequently one of the biggest problems faced in contemporary print design is matching the colour represented on screen with the colour printed on paper as there will always be a discrepancy between what we see on screen and what we see printed. The computer can only simulate the results of printed colour therefore the colour transmitted on a monitor will never accurately represent the reflected colour on a printed page. Numerous factors affect this fidelity that must be considered for accurate results.

The quality of the RGB prediction of the CMYK output depends in part on the quality of the display. This can alter not only according to the quality of the monitor, its calibration, the computer's graphics card and operating system, but it also varies between design programs. As displays will vary it is important to print hard proofs of designs to achieve a more accurate preview of how the colours will look in the final print run. It is most likely today, in the office and at home, that designers will use an inkjet printer to produce these proofs. The quality of these prints is also subject to a number of factors. Colour fidelity will vary between printer make and model, but more importantly between ink cartridge manufacturer and model, and the quality of paper stock being printed on.

In order to have more control over the fidelity of your inkjet proof, custom settings should be used to manually adjust levels of each of the three primary colours and the contrast of black each time a new document is produced. It is fundamental to understand that what is printed, whether at home or at a professional press, will not be true to what is previewed on screen, and what is previewed on screen will not be true to what is printed.

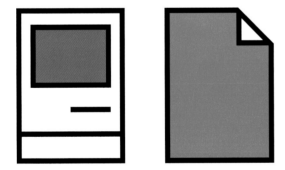

DIGITALLY MIXING IN CMYK MODE

This book details the mixing of primary colours in printer's inks, and for this the CMYK mode must be used. Vector-based packages such as Freehand and Illustrator work in the same way when mixing CMYK. In the colour mixing panel values can be entered numerically in the percentage fields or by dragging the sliders. The swatch box will automatically be updated to indicate the result.

To prevent potential muddiness – the result of too much of each colour being mixed together – the sum of the components of the process colours should never exceed 240%. A colour comprising 30% cyan, 10% magenta, and 60% yellow (= 100%) is fine (1), but one containing 70% cyan, 100% magenta, and 80% yellow (= 250%) will not be as clear on the actual print as it may appear on screen and will be hard to distinguish from black (2).

Colours mixed in this mode are referred to as 'process'. Process colours involve four printing plates for outputting on a printing press, while a spot colour has its own dedicated plate as it is printed as a separate ink. Spot colours are special inks that are used when a colour required is beyond the range of the four printing inks (for example silver), or when a specific colour must be reproduced accurately over a range of materials (for example a corporate colour). Spot colours should be kept to a minimum as each colour will require a new printing plate, increasing printing costs.

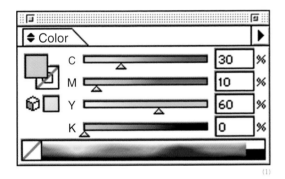

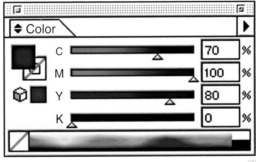

(1)

(2)

THE COLOUR WHEEL

Essential to the foundation of any aesthetic colour theory
is the colour wheel as it determines the classification and
organisation of colours.

A basic colour wheel will consist of the three primary colours.
These are considered to be absolute mixtures that cannot be
created by mixing any other colours, but can produce almost
any other colour when mixed. As has been discussed, in print
these colours are cyan, magenta, and yellow (1).

A colour wheel including secondary colours (the result of
mixing primaries two at a time in equal amounts (2)) will
include six colours. A wheel that includes tertiary hues
(the result of mixing a primary with a secondary (3)) will
include twelve colours. Although with the precision of
digital colour mixing, it is possible that a colour wheel
could continue this trend to produce thousands of barely
distinguishable colours, the twelve-colour wheel shows
the roots of all other colours (4).

When mixing secondary colours using paint, it is hard to
balance the mixture perfectly so that it leans to neither side
of the parent colour. Secondary orange for example, must not
contain too much magenta or too much yellow. This is not a
problem faced by the designer today. Although the principle
must be kept in mind, values can be entered mathematically
and therefore with extreme precision.

The principles of mixing colour with the CMYK palette
are similar to those of physically mixing pigment or paint:
different percentages of each primary are mixed automatically
to create a flawless and instantly repeatable colour mix.

It is vital that you experiment with these principles of mixing
colour and the colour wheel. Whether it is in the form of a
wheel is not important, but an attempt should be made to
create secondary and tertiary hues. Experience through
practice is the best way to learn about and to become
proficient in colour mixing.

(1)

(3)

(2)

(4)

MIXING GREYS

It is often thought that greys are best produced with a
mixture of black and white. In fact, the most effective
greys are the product of mixing two contrasting hues (1)
or the three primary hues in equal parts (2), with the addition
of black or white to enhance the mixture if required. Mixing
grey in this way will result in a far warmer and deeper grey
than simply using a mix of black and white.

Mixing black with white pigment in varying proportions
produces a range of greys. Black and white, along with
these greys, are known as neutral colours. Although
countless steps of grey can be produced it is easiest
to create nine and categorise them into three groups.
Dark greys = 90% black to 70% black (3)
Middle greys = 60% to 40% black (4)
Light greys = 30% to 10% black (5)

It is important to study gradation by producing greyscales
as they demonstrate a gradual stepping up or down between
white and black, light and dark. This helps us develop an
eye for the differences between lighter and darker value in
different hues.

DIMENSIONS OF COLOUR

Apart from the relative positions of colours on the colour wheel, their quantitative proportion and their degrees of purity and brilliance are also important. The first step in exploring colour is to use all possible variations of a single hue.

Hue describes the position of a colour on the colour wheel and is used to name the colour, for instance 'red' or 'magenta' (1). It is not to be confused with colour. Variations within a hue create different colours, but the hue remains the same. As well as hue, elemental to any discussion of colour are the terms value, and chroma. *Value* describes the lightness or darkness of a colour, its position on a scale from white to black (2). *Chroma* refers to the brightness, saturation and impact of a colour. It is the difference between brilliant and dull (3). (In other texts and computer packages this third dimension of colour may well be referred to as saturation.)

These three qualities are known as the three different dimensions that can be applied to each colour. An understanding of and familiarity with these dimensions is important as the manipulation of a hue's value and chroma can result in a range of over 20 colours.

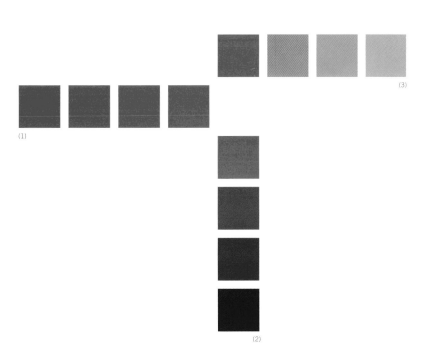

(1)

(2)

(3)

VALUE

Of all the colour contrasts, value can be used most
significantly. Value changes can be made by mixing
a colour with white or black in varying proportions (1).
Value can either be manipulated to maintain maximum
chroma or to suppress it. In order to manipulate value and
maintain maximum chroma a hue must be of considerable
brilliance. The manipulation of value with minimum chroma
makes the hue barely identifiable.

By adding lots of white to a palette in design we create tints
of colour. In keeping the value light without losing any colour
definition, the design is known as high key (2).

By adding greys, the intensity of colour is quietened and
the value deepened. The design becomes less bright and
is known as middle key. There is a danger that too much
grey will quieten the colours and it is a challenge to keep
the colours fresh (3).

By adding black to our colour palette, we create shades
of colours and take the value range much deeper. The
intensity of the colours can be totally muted and this is
known as low key (4).

For budgetary reasons graphic designers will often have to
work with a limited palette, perhaps only one or two colours
of printed ink on a white ground. If, in this case, the designer
needs to give the appearance of more variety in colour, value
gradations can be used.

(1)

(2)

(3)

(4)

COMPUTER PALETTE VALUE ADJUSTMENTS

Making adjustments to the value of a hue by creating a shade in a computer program is very straightforward. Having defined a colour in either Freehand or Illustrator the addition of a shade is quite clear. The black colour bar below the cyan, magenta, and yellow levels can be adjusted to increase the amount of black to the colour mix. This adjusts the level of shade to a hue.

However, there is no slider to add white to the mix. The two packages approach the creation of tints in different ways. In Freehand, once a colour has been mixed it is relatively easy to create a tint (1).
1. Open the tint panel by choosing Window > Panel > Tints.
2. Choose the tint amount of the selected colour mix by adjusting the slider, typing in a percentage, or clicking one of the tint swatches in the panel.
3. The tint can then be dragged into the Swatch List for use.

In Illustrator the process is a little different (2). Before creating a tint of a selected colour, the colour must first be specified as either process or spot.
1. Having mixed a colour as shown previously, drag it into the swatches panel.
2. Select it and choose Swatch Options in the swatches pop-up menu. (Click the triangle at the top right-hand corner of the swatch panel to access this menu.) The Swatch Options dialog box will be displayed.
3. Choose either Process or Spot. Click OK.
4. The bottom right-hand corner of the square swatch will now appear cropped and the CMYK colour bars in the colour panel will have been replaced by one bar labelled T. This is the Tint Shader. Adjustments to the level of tint can now be made by dragging the slider or typing in a percentage. By switching mode back to CMYK – by clicking on the triangle at the top right corner of the colour panel and selecting CMYK – shades can be added again.

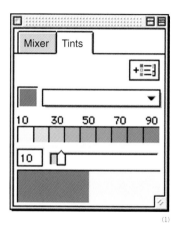

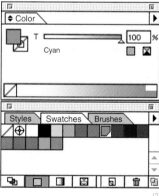

(1)

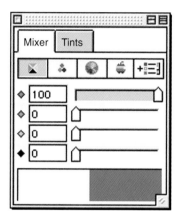

(2)

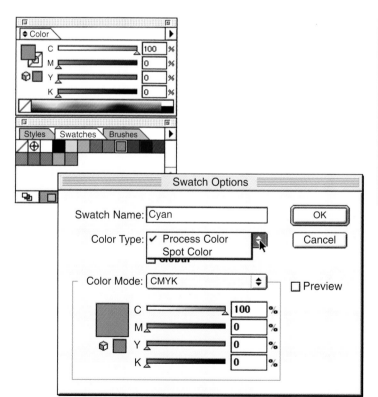

CHROMA

Colours with strong chroma are the most brilliant and vivid colours that can be obtained. Colours with weak chroma are dull and appear to contain a large proportion of grey.

A good way of demonstrating and understanding chroma is to mix any two hues to create a range of hue gradations. If the two chosen hues are close to each other on the colour wheel, and correctly biased, the mixtures will maintain considerable chroma strength (1). If not, the result will be a weaker chroma mixture. When hues opposite each other on the colour wheel are mixed, chroma is significantly reduced (2).

(1)

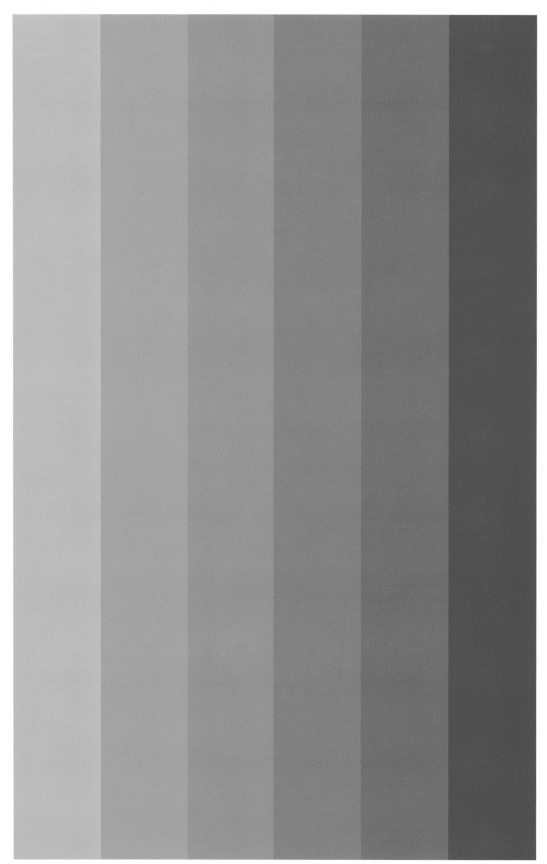

(2)

SYSTEMATIC PRINCIPLES
HARMONY

RANGE EXPLORATION

It is important that we experiment with the value and chroma
of a hue as it makes us aware and knowledgeable of the full
range of colours that are at our disposal. This knowledge can
then help take colour use beyond unconscious preferences,
help in times of restriction and add an accomplished
aesthetic to a design.

HARMONY

COLOUR HARMONY

Colour harmony is created by colour combinations that
work well together and hence successfully please the eye.
Everyone has their individual taste and therefore his or her
idea of what a pleasing colour scheme is; this is known as
subjective opinion. Palettes chosen solely according to the
designer's personal preference are what we call subjective
colour. This is the subject matter explored in the second
section of this book. It is impossible to develop specific
rules for the creation of subjective colour combinations that
effectively please everyone as tastes change from generation
to generation and in accordance to a person's age, sex, race,
education etc. Colour harmony is consequently best and most
reliably created systematically.

DEVELOPING A COLOUR SCHEME SYSTEMATICALLY

The colour scheme refers to the colours that are selected for a design. In most cases, a colour scheme will consist of more than one hue. For example, a hue that plays a dominant role in a design may be accompanied by a subordinate hue to provide contrast and accent. The success of a design can depend largely on the harmony between the colours chosen for a scheme.

If a design is required to please a large audience colour harmony is best created according to established and fail-safe theories of selection based on the position of colours on the colour wheel. This tool of organisation is indispensable in showing the basic organisation and interrelationships of colours, and in aiding colour selection. It is fundamental that anyone who works with colours is familiar with the colour wheel. Colour selections derived from the colour wheel systems guarantee a successful end result by creating harmonious schemes that can also have the added benefit of creating various optical effects.

MONOCHROME

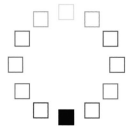

The simplest colour scheme is achieved when a single hue
is used with variations in value added to it (1). This is known
as monochrome. It is possible to break up the unity of a
monochromatic scheme by using neutral colours; whites,
blacks, and greys (2).

If a tight production budget is imposed monochrome printing
can substantially reduce printing costs. One can use extreme
tonal contrasts and many tints and shades of colour to
overcome the limitations of the print. By using only tints
of one colour in a design only one plate will need to be
used as the white comes from the paper and not an extra
white ink; if you want to add shades, however, an extra ink
(black) will be needed.

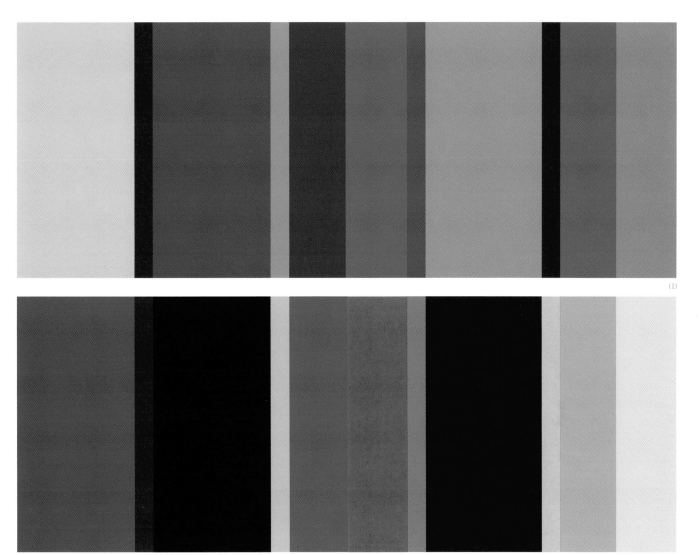

(1)

(2)

ANALOGOUS

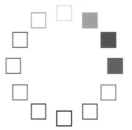

A scheme can be harmonious when the colours chosen are
close to each other on the colour wheel and therefore alike in
appearance. These are analogous colours. When more than
two analogous colours are selected from the colour wheel, the
colour positioned in the middle is known as the 'ruling colour'
as it can most easily alter its neighbours. These generally
express a soft harmony, as they stress similarities rather
than differences between hues.

Analogous selections can also be achieved by mixing a tiny quantity of one colour into every colour in the scheme. This technique can be used to add unity by creating an overall tone to a colour scheme which may otherwise seem disparate. For example, adding a hint of yellow to a scheme of randomly selected colours will make the scheme appear more unified, as shown here.

COMPLEMENTS

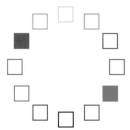

Hues that are directly opposite each other on the colour
wheel are known as complementary hues. Although there
is some contrast between any two hues, complementary
hues exhibit the strongest hue contrast. Contrast between
complementary hues is greatest if the hues are of the
same value. These hues provide a mutual and perfectly
level balance and also intensify each other's appearance
with a stimulating result. Toning down the saturation
or raising or lowering their value will lessen the contrast
between complementary colours, but they may still
intensify each other's liveliness.

(1)

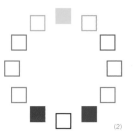

(2)

When two hues adjacent to each other on the colour wheel are used with their respective complements, we get a double complementary (1).

A split-complementary scheme uses hues that are either side of a dominant hue's complement on the colour wheel. These hues establish a multicoloured scheme with both analogous and contrasting relationships. The contrast here is softer than a complementary pair (2).

Hues that are not precisely 180 degrees apart from each other on the colour wheel are known as near-complementary hues and have a similar effect to complementary hues but with less contrast (3).

A mutual complement is made with one dominant colour, its complement, and the two hues not directly next to, but the next ones either side of the complement. All three colours on the opposite side to the dominant colour can be used in conjunction with the dominant colour (4).

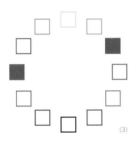

(3)

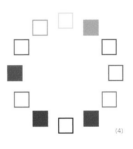

(4)

TRIADS

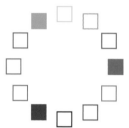

A broad range of contrast is seen in a triad colour scheme.
These draw on three hues equidistant from each other on the
colour wheel. The imaginary equilateral triangle that connects
these hues can be rotated within the wheel connecting any
other group of three equidistant colours.

SYSTEMATIC PRINCIPLES
HARMONY

CHROMA AND VALUE HARMONY

It is possible that any number of hues can be chosen from the colour wheel at random to create an effective colour scheme, provided that value and chroma are suitably manipulated. The resulting colours can lead to unusual palettes as even though the hues are unrelated, they appear to belong together.

When the hues have been determined, value and chroma adjustments and variations should be considered. Chroma harmony can be achieved by using colours that have the same degree of chroma strength, analogous chroma (1). A design using full chroma colours will have emphasis on hue contrast, whereas weak chroma throughout will neutralise contrast. Alternatively it may be decided that the composition is to be of high or low key, uniform value (2), maximum chroma or minimum chroma, before the hues are chosen.

(1)

(2)

WARM–COOL CONTRAST

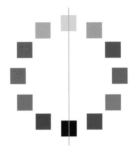

In western tradition colours can be used to describe our emotions; angry = red, sad = blue, envy = green. However, these associations may not necessarily translate across to other cultures. One universally understood meaning of colour is the sensation of temperature. Not only can colours provide contrasts such as light and dark, but also warm and cool. Reds, oranges and yellows appear warm and blues cool.

The relative temperature of a colour can be classified according to its position on the colour wheel. If, on the colour wheel, yellow is placed at the top and its complementary purple is placed at the bottom, we can vertically divide the wheel into two halves. The colours on the left appear warm, and the colours on the right, the blue side, appear cool. With this division it becomes clear that not all yellows are necessarily warm as the ones that fall on the blue side appear cooler than those that fall on the left. Balance of mixture shows that distinctions between warm

and cool can be subtle. For example, a blue can be made warmer by adding a hint of red and vice versa. A grey can also be warm or cool with the addition of a hue from the appropriate side of the colour wheel.

The warmth or coolness of a colour also depends on its context and what lies next to it. The same hue may seem warm when placed next to a cooler colour or cool if it is placed next to a colour that appears warmer (see opposite).

If warm colours are used for an entire design it will obviously appear warmer than a design which uses cool colours. If a blue, or red tint, is added to all of the colours in a palette then the palette will also appear relatively warmer or cooler. Systematic colour selections made according to temperature will effectively result in a harmonious scheme.

CONCLUSION

It has become clear that certain systematic colour combinations provide harmony, and help the designer choose colour schemes that will definitely please the eyes of the audience. Knowledge of the principles of colour use in design as detailed in this section of the book need not restrict the designer, and can be a great help in times of indecision. These principles may seem like dogmatic laws but the choices made can still be influenced according to personal preference or subject matter. As creatives it is inevitable that we will at times prefer to use expressive freedom in our colour selection and discard established systems. In this case it is important to understand the effects of the relationships that arbitrary colour selections can cause.

SYSTEMATIC / SUBJECTIVE
COLOUR SELECTION

An AVA Book
Published by AVA Publishing SA
c/o Fidinter SA
Ch. de la Joliette 2
Case postale 96
1000 Lausanne 6
Switzerland
Tel: +41 786 005 109
Email: enquiries@avabooks.ch

Distributed by Thames and Hudson
(ex-North America)
181a High Holborn
London WC1V 7QX
United Kingdom
Tel: +44 20 7845 5000
Fax: +44 20 7845 5055
Email: sales@thameshudson.co.uk
www.thamesandhudson.com

Distributed by Sterling Publishing Co., Inc.
in the USA
387 Park Avenue South
New York, NY 10016-8810
Tel: +1 212 532 7160
Fax: +1 212 213 2495
www.sterlingpub.com

in Canada
Sterling Publishing
c/o Canadian Manda Group
One Atlantic Avenue, Suite 105
Toronto, Ontario M6K 3E7

English Language Support Office
AVA Publishing (UK) Ltd.
Tel: +44 1903 204 455
Email: enquiries@avabooks.co.uk

ISBN 2-88479-057-8

10 9 8 7 6 5 4 3 2 1

Written and designed by
Andrew Bellamy
Typeset in Trade Gothic and Univers

Production and separations by AVA
Book Production Pte. Ltd., Singapore
Tel: +65 6334 8173
Fax: +65 6334 0752
Email: production@avabooks.com.sg

AVA Publishing SA
Switzerland

SYSTEMATIC / SUBJECTIVE

COLOUR SELECTION

Andrew Bellamy

HOW TO GET THE MOST FROM THIS BOOK

The topics in this book are clearly identified and dedicated generous space so the information can easily be accessed at random. The book is divided into two clear sections as each section covers a different method of colour selection. However, a foundation of knowledge is built in *Systematic Colour Selection* that is referenced in *Subjective Colour Selection*. It is therefore recommended that those with a basic knowledge of colour read *Systematic Colour Selection* first.

The navigation bar at the bottom of each page allows you to see exactly where you are in the book by listing each section and its content divisions in order. The darker type indicates which section and topic division you are in, while the lighter type indicates what has come before and what comes after (see example below). This is particularly useful if you choose to access the book at random as it allows you to quickly and easily locate your position in the book in relation to the rest of the content.

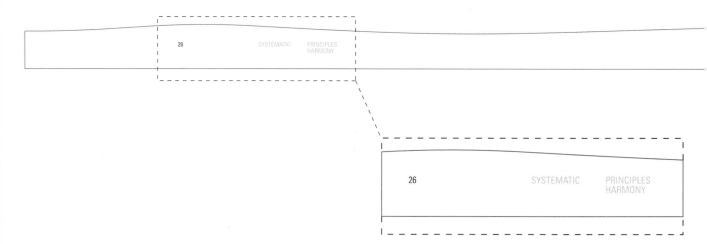

SUBJECTIVE   PHENOMENA
             EFFECTS
             APPENDIX   27

SUBJECTIVE   PHENOMENA
             EFFECTS
             APPENDIX   27

This indicates that you are in the Effects
section of *Subjective Colour Selection*.

CONTENTS

SYSTEMATIC PRINCIPLES
HARMONY

INTRODUCTION

The first section of this book deals with the choice of harmonious colour selections made according to systems based around the colour wheel. Whether colours are combined according to established colour schemes or not, one must be aware of the optical effects that are caused by the interaction of adjacent colours. This is vital as colours are rarely seen in isolation. Colours are surrounded by other colours, and they all interact in our perception.

Many factors can affect the way that we perceive a specific hue and it is essential to note that a colour's appearance is conditional and cannot be judged outside of its environment. One colour will have many different readings depending on its surroundings and therefore must always be seen in relation to them.

The way that juxtapositions of specific colours affect our perception must be studied and understood so the resulting effects can be avoided or exploited accordingly. This is especially important when selecting colours subjectively: *Subjective Colour Selection* provides a comprehensive guide to the cause and results of these effects.

PHENOMENA

AFTER-IMAGE

Since we almost never see a colour in an environment where it is unrelated to any others, it is important to understand how colours affect each other, and how they can alter each other's appearance. Our sight can deceive us into seeing one colour as a different colour when placed in different contexts, or on different backgrounds. To help understand why colours can be read differently to how they physically are we must first understand after-image.

Also known as successive contrasts, after-images occur in our visual perception all the time. However, we are not usually aware of the phenomenon. The after-image of a colour can be made clearly visible and apparent if we place a small square of it on a white background. If, having stared at the colour for some time, our gaze is shifted to a blank area of the white, we see a phantom of its shape which should theoretically be in the complementary hue. This phantom complement can also be seen if, rather than shift our gaze, we continue to stare intensely at the chosen shape. In this case a glow of the complementary hue can appear around the shape's boundaries. However, this is only a rough guide. For example, the after-image of a square of magenta will appear green, but will not be identical to the green that is its complement on the colour wheel. Black and white can also be seen as complementary colours, with black producing an after-image of white and vice versa. This shows that not only hue, but value affect this phenomenon as shades produce light, and tints produce dark after-images.

Simultaneous contrast is an effect of after-image and occurs most readily when a colour is encompassed by another. The term refers to the apparent changes in hue, value and/or chroma that are created by adjacent colours. This is caused by the eye's generation of the after-image that is of the complementary colour to the original image. When combining colours we must pay attention to the effects of simultaneous contrast as it can alter the way colours are perceived.

For example, when an orange square is surrounded by cyan, the after-image of cyan (its complement red) tints the orange and makes it appear to contain more red (1). If the same orange is surrounded by purple it is tinted by the after-image of purple, which is yellow, making it appear more yellow (2).

If a small square of grey that doesn't hint at any colour (neutral) is placed in a surrounding colour, the grey will be tinged by the complementary of the chosen encompassing hue (3). This effect can be enhanced or neutralised by the use of a slightly coloured grey. On an orange background, a bluish grey will intensify the effect, but an orange grey will counteract the illusory modification (4).

This is illustrated on the following spread where there are three different greys on an orange background. The first grey contains a hint of blue which becomes intensified due to simultaneous contrast. The grey in the middle is neutral, but appears to contain a hint of blue, the complementary of the surrounding orange. And finally the grey on the right contains a hint of orange, but this is neutralised by the effect of simultaneous contrast making it appear chromatically unbiased.

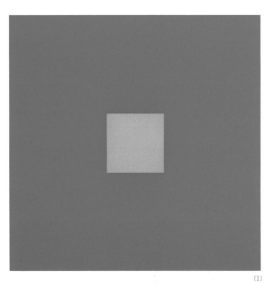

(1)

(2)

(3)

SYSTEMATIC   PRINCIPLES
HARMONY

(4)

CHANGE OF VALUE IN SIMULTANEOUS CONTRAST

Value changes due to simultaneous contrast occur when
the surrounding colour is significantly lighter or darker
than the central colour. If the surrounding colour is light the
inner colour appears darker as it is shaded by a dark after-
image (1). The same principle applies to a dark background
but with the opposite effect. If the surrounding colour is dark
the central colour appears lighter as it is tinted by a light
after-image (2).

CHANGE OF CHROMA IN SIMULTANEOUS CONTRAST

When a colour is surrounded by its complementary the chroma of the central colour is increased as it is enhanced by the same hue as itself. This is because the after-image of the surrounding colour is the centre's complementary (3). Thus the central colour becomes more radiant and can appear to glow. If a light colour is to appear dramatically luminous, it is a good idea to juxtapose it with a dark surround (2).

When two colours being related are within 90 degrees of each other in the colour circle simultaneous contrast weakens chroma (4). Take for example orange surrounded by red. The after-image of green produced by the red will grey the orange in the centre. The green cast has a neutralising effect.

(1)

(2)
>

(3)

SYSTEMATIC PRINCIPLES
HARMONY

(4)

EFFECTS

DEPTH

The illusion of depth in design can be achieved not only
by the composition of elements but also by colour selection.
Illusions of depth can be created on flat surfaces by using
colours that advance or recede depending on the context
of the adjacent or surrounding colours.

SPATIAL ADVANCE AND RECESSION

Distance, nearness, and equidistance between colours can therefore be achieved by the comparison and distinction of colour boundaries. Softer boundaries imply connection and therefore nearness; harder boundaries accentuate separation and therefore indicate distance (1). For example, on a white background light tones are held down by their close connection to the plane of the ground, and shades approaching black are driven forward as the boundary lines are sharply defined. On a black background the opposite is true. Dark shades are held down by soft boundaries, and light shades are thrust forward by hard boundaries (2). Middle mixtures often appear as meeting on a two-dimensional plane as their boundaries are equally soft or hard. Given these effects colours can therefore be read as above or below each other.

Apparent spatial advancing or receding can be controlled by contrast between colour boundaries. This can be explained by the fact that hue and value contrasts appear great in things close to us, and less apparent in things seen at a distance.

(1)
>

SYSTEMATIC   PRINCIPLES
HARMONY

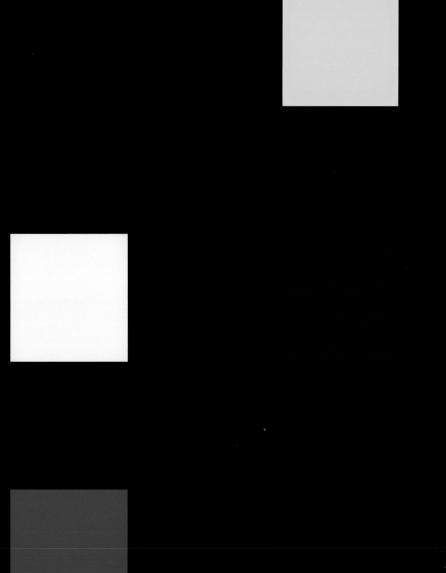

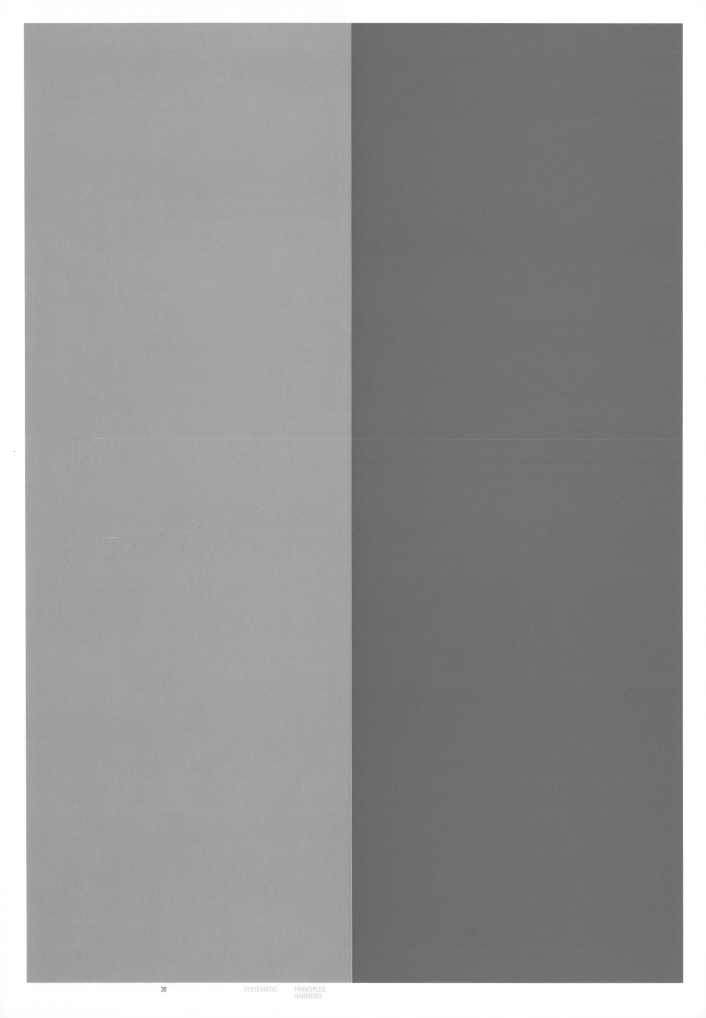

SYSTEMATIC PRINCIPLES
HARMONY

WARM–COOL DISTANCE

Warm–cool sensations also affect the illusion of depth in
design as warm hues appear to advance and cool hues
recede. The warmth or coolness of elements in design can
therefore be used to effectively express space and depth.

Among cold and warm hues of equal chroma, the warm will
advance and the cold will retreat. However, these effects can
be cancelled out with appropriate alteration to the hue's
value. If a blue is lightened enough it can be made to appear
at the same level or in front of a warm red (1). The blue can
also appear to be in front of the red if the red is darkened,
pushing it below the blue (2).

(1)   (2)

DISTANCE AND SIZE OF COLOURED AREA

The size of a coloured area of a design can also affect
distance. The increase in the amount of colour that covers
a printed area visually reduces distance as the viewer's
vision is flooded with colour and results in the effect
of nearness. Small areas of colour can appear far away
as they are less dominant.

SIZE OF COLOURED AREA AND CHROMA

The size of a coloured area does not only affect nearness, but also chroma. A large expanse of colour will generally appear brighter than a very small area of the same colour. However, this can only be used as a rough guide as the effect depends heavily on the colour of the surrounding area. It is equally possible that with a dark background the opposite will be true. One must become aware of the effect with experience through experimentation.

SIZE

Colour can affect the apparent size of elements in a design. For example, areas of brighter colour generally leap out at the viewer and consequently seem larger than static darker colours of identical size and shape. However, it is impossible to develop concrete rules that predict the perception of the apparent changes in size of coloured elements as the possible relationships between value, position, and background are countless and all affect the fragmentary rules.

It is important to simply be aware that apparent changes in size caused by colour are possible. For example, on the right the white square on the black background appears larger than the black square of the same size on the white background. The white of the top square reaches out and overflows its boundaries whereas the black square's boundaries are flooded by the white of the ground and hence the shape appears to contract. The relating elements of each of the illustrations on this spread are identical in size and are designed to demonstrate illusory changes in size. You need to develop an eye for these changes through experience rather than learn the causes and effects that are entirely relative.

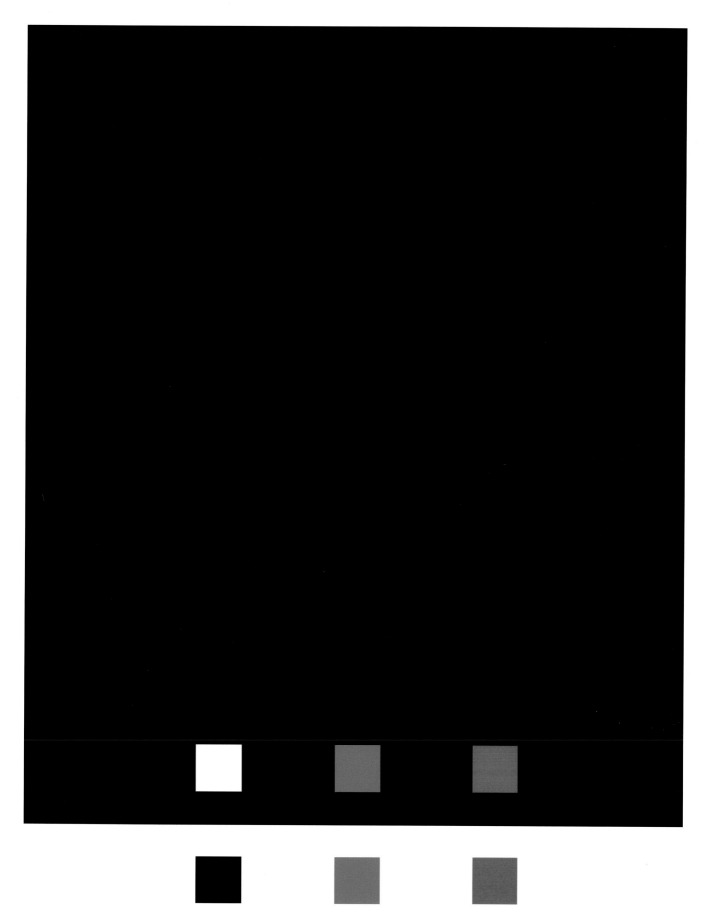

VIBRATING AND VANISHING BOUNDARIES

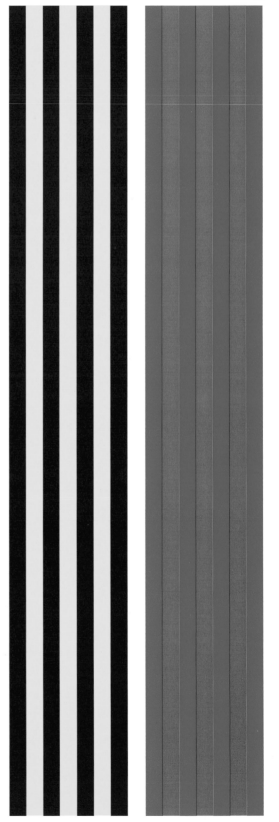

Vibrating boundaries can be seen in colours which are
contrasting in their hues. When areas of contrasting colours
are juxtaposed the boundary lives between them often appear
duplicated giving an awkward sense of movement (1 & 2).
This movement creates an uncomfortable and aggressive
effect on the eye and should be avoided if harmony is the
aim. The effect can, however, be successfully exploited as an
eye-catching device as the coloured elements appear to move
and leap out at the viewer.

Boundaries can also be rendered unrecognisable or invisible
through the choice of colour alone. This creates the opposite
effect to the vibrating boundaries and cannot work with
very contrasting hues. It is confined to neighbouring
(analogous) colours (3).

The effect depends most decisively on equality in value.
If colours of equal value or very similar hue are juxtaposed,
it is hard to discern where one colour stops and the other
starts. The effect of their interaction is vanishing boundaries.
Contrasting hues have to be of very high or low value for their
boundaries to vanish (4 & 5). This effect is very easy to
produce with colours of very high and very low value.
With highly saturated middle values, colours must be very
close in hue to lose the edge between them (6 & 7). Edges
of forms become soft and indefinable when there is little
colour contrast between them, whereas edges of highly
contrasting hues are hard and sharply defined.

(3)   (4)   (5)   (6)   (7)

SYSTEMATIC   PRINCIPLES
                                        HARMONY

PARASITES

It is important to be aware that certain colours can drain
energy from their neighbours. Dull tones, especially greys,
feed from the strength of any vivid colours around them.
We can observe this by placing a neutral grey and a vivid
colour in an alternately repetitive pattern. The grey will be
seen to take on the vividness of the interspersed chromatic
colour which now appears reduced and comparatively
weakened. This draining effect must be avoided if a key
hue is to appear at its maximum potential strength.

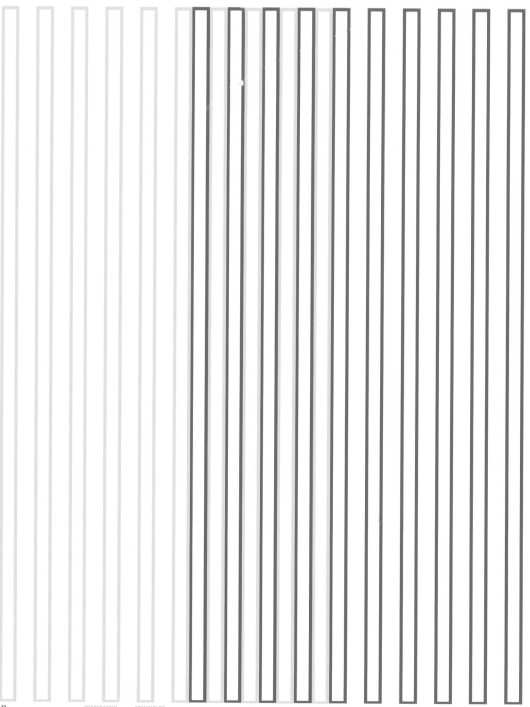

SYSTEMATIC   PRINCIPLES
HARMONY

PROJECTED COLOUR

In some cases, colours can appear to project themselves
out of their physical boundaries to tint larger neutral areas
in their own hue. Colours with strong chroma and light value
such as yellow are the most effective at producing projected
colour, but the effect is dependant on the strength and
definition of boundary lines. Colours that are furthest away
from the background in hue and value have hard and well
defined boundary lines that contain the projection more
effectively than those with soft boundary divisions. However,
like a bright light brilliant chroma can appear to project itself
beyond any boundary.

OPTICAL MIX

Another of colour's illusory qualities is that of optical mixture;
optical as the colours are mixed by the eye and not physically
in pigment. Here, two colours (or more) perceived
simultaneously are seen combined and therefore mixed
into a new colour. In this process, the two original colours
are cancelled out and replaced by the new optical mixture.
For example, an illusion of the green on the left can be
produced by a repetitive pattern of tightly packed yellow
and cyan lines (right). The quality of the effect and the size
of the elements used are dependant on the distance that the
design will be seen from the viewer. If the design will be held
close to the eyes, the elements of the pattern creating the
mix have to be extremely small. These elements can increase
in size according to an increase in distance between the
design and the viewer.

CONCLUSION

As has been seen there are numerous conditions that affect
our perception of a single colour or colour scheme. A group
of colours, therefore, that work well in one design may not
work well in another as the elements of the design such as
shape and composition will be different. The position of the
colours, the size of the areas they fill, relation to their ground
and the effects of simultaneous contrast must all be
considered when creating any colour scheme. It is
important to understand these principles so the effects
can be predicted allowing us to avoid or exploit them to
create specific, deliberate and successful designs.

APPENDIX

SYSTEMATIC PRINCIPLES
HARMONY

POSTER CARDS

The pages that follow provide examples of the properties of
colour and how colour can be used to maximum effect in
design. They are perforated so please remove and exhibit
them on the wall of your class, studio or home as a source
of inspiration and as helpful reminders.

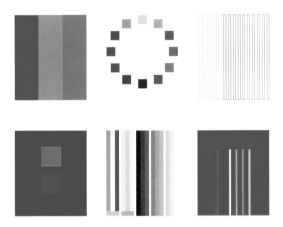

OPTICAL MIX

OPTICAL MIX

One of colour's illusory qualities is that of optical mixture.
Optical as the colours are mixed in the eye and not physically
in pigment. Here, two colours (or more) perceived
simultaneously are seen combined and therefore mixed
into a new colour. This can be a particularly useful tool
when the designer is restricted to a limited colour palette.
If only two colours are allowed but three are required for
a design, optical mix can be used to create the illusion of
a third colour. More details of optical mix and colour's full
potential in design can be found in *Systematic / Subjective
Colour Selection*.

Andrew Bellamy
ISBN: 2-88479-057-8
Available from all good bookshops

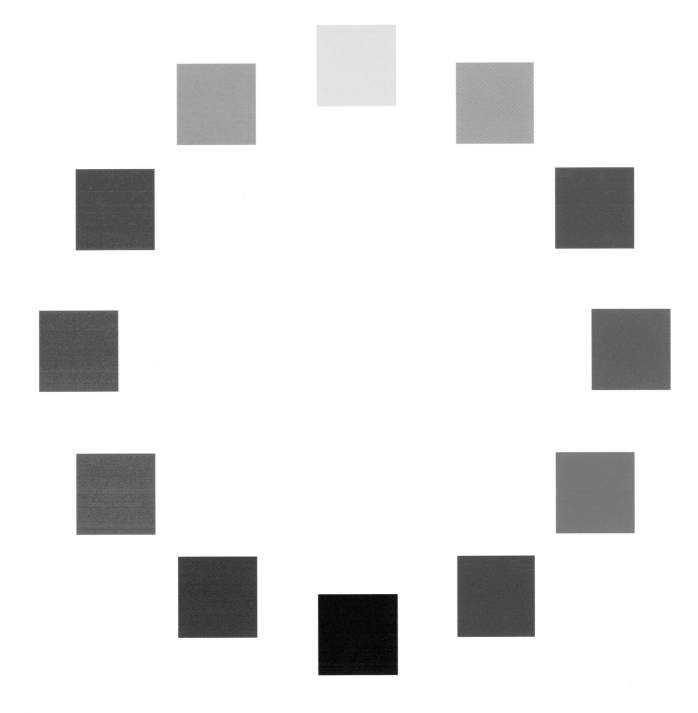

THE COLOUR WHEEL

SYSTEMATIC / SUBJECTIVE
COLOUR SELECTION

THE COLOUR WHEEL

Essential to the foundation of any aesthetic colour theory is
the colour wheel as it determines the classification of colours.
A basic colour wheel will consist of the three primary colours,
three secondary colours, and six tertiary hues. The twelve-
colour wheel is at the root of all other colours. It is vital that
you actually experiment with these principles of mixing colour
and the colour wheel. It is a good idea for a designer to
always have a colour wheel in sight when designing as it
can aid effective colour mixing and selection. More details
of the colour wheel and colour's full potential in design can
be found in *Systematic / Subjective Colour Selection.*

Andrew Bellamy
ISBN: 2-88479-057-8
Available from all good bookshops

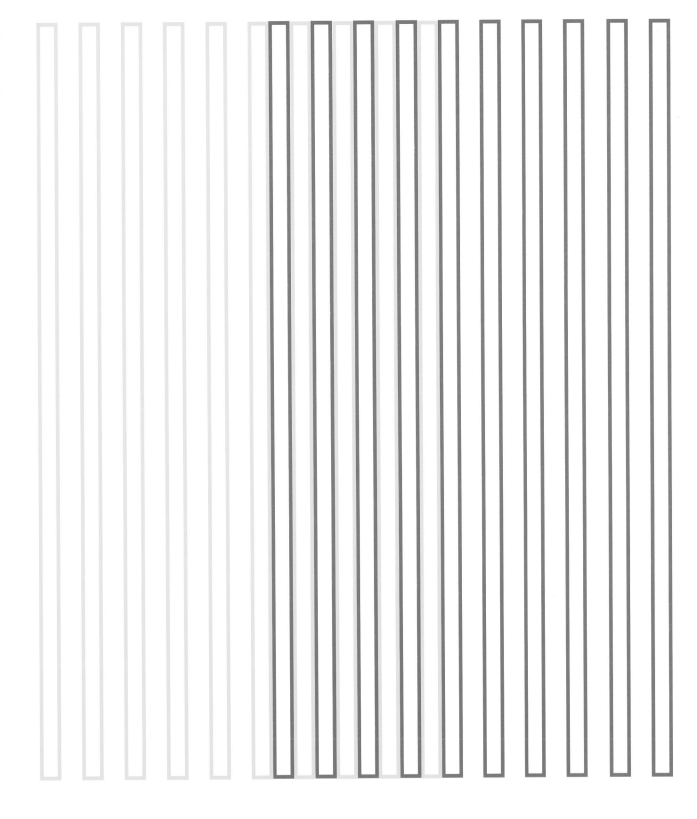

PROJECTED COLOUR

SYSTEMATIC / SUBJECTIVE
COLOUR SELECTION

PROJECTED COLOUR

In some cases, colours can appear to project themselves out
of their physical boundaries to tint larger neutral areas. Here,
the blue and yellow areas tint the white space in their own
hue, but where they overlap the white is tinged with green,
an optical mix. It is important to be aware of this effect so
that it can be avoided or exploited accordingly. If a limited
amount of colours are allowed for, the effect could be used
to give the illusion of large areas of tints of colour and more
colours than are apparent. More details of projected colour
and colour's full potential in design can be found in
Systematic / Subjective Colour Selection.

Andrew Bellamy
ISBN: 2-88479-057-8
Available from all good bookshops

SIMULTANEOUS CONTRAST

COLOUR SELECTION

SYSTEMATIC / SUBJECTIVE
COLOUR SELECTION

SIMULTANEOUS CONTRAST

When combining colours we must pay attention to the effects
of simultaneous contrast as it can alter the way colours are
perceived. Simultaneous contrast refers to the apparent
changes in hue, value and/or chroma that are created by
adjacent colours. This happens most when a colour is
altered by a colour that surrounds it and can be used as
a sensational eye-catching tool. It is important to understand
this effect so the result can be predicted, controlled and
used effectively. More details of simultaneous contrast and
colour's full potential in design can be found in *Systematic /
Subjective Colour Selection.*

Andrew Bellamy
ISBN: 2-88479-057-8
Available from all good bookshops

GREYS

COLOUR SELECTION

SYSTEMATIC / SUBJECTIVE
COLOUR SELECTION

GREYS

Greys can be achieved by mixing black with white pigment in varying proportions to produce a scale of greys, but also from mixing two contrasting hues or the three primary hues in equal parts, with the addition of black or white to enhance the mixture if required. These mixtures result in deeper, warmer, and more attractive greys. Black and white, along with these greys, are known as neutral colours. More details of the use of greys and colour's full potential in design can be found in *Systematic / Subjective Colour Selection*.

Andrew Bellamy
ISBN: 2-88479-057-8
Available from all good bookshops

DEPTH

SYSTEMATIC / SUBJECTIVE
COLOUR SELECTION

DEPTH

The illusion of depth in design is not only attributed to the composition of the subject but also the colour. Illusions of depth can be created on flat surfaces by using colours that advance or recede depending on the context of the adjacent or surrounding colours. Distance, nearness, and equidistance between colours can be achieved by the comparison and distinction of colour boundaries. These effects can be very useful in creating hierarchy in a design and guiding the viewer's eye. More details of the illusion of depth and colour's full potential in design can be found in *Systematic / Subjective Colour Selection*.

Andrew Bellamy
ISBN: 2-88479-057-8
Available from all good bookshops

GLOSSARY

Additive colour
Colours in transmitted light that become lighter in value when mixed with additional colours.

After-image
The phenomena of apparent colour complements and shapes that occur in the eye and are visible having stared at a colour for some time and then looked away.

Analogous colours
Colours that are similar to each other and therefore positioned closely on the colour wheel.

Cathode Ray Tube
CRT, device used by most computer monitors to display images by emitting electron beams to excite phosphors that coat the inside of the screen.

Chroma
The brilliance, saturation and impact of a colour.

CMYK
Cyan, magenta, yellow, and key (black): the four-colour printing process used to create and print all other printable colours.

Colour mixing panel
The panel in a computer program that allows the precise definition of colour levels and colour mix.

Colour wheel
Device used to show the classification, organisation, and interrelationships of colours.

Complementary colours
Hues that are diametrically opposite each other on the colour wheel.

Electron gun
Device used by most computer monitors to produce a narrow stream of electrons from a heated cathode.

Gradation
The gradual transition between one shade, tone, or colour to another.

High key
The term given to a palette that contains a lot of white.

Hue
Name attributed to a colour to describe its position in the spectrum or on the colour wheel to help discern it from another colour.

Low key
The term given to a palette that contains a lot of black.

Middle key
The term given to a palette that contains a lot of grey.

Monochrome

When only a single hue and variations in value are used for a colour scheme.

Optical mixture

When adjacent colours blend in the eye to create an apparent mixture that is not present in the pigment.

Palette

A tool for mixing colour or a term for a selection of colours used in a design.

Parasites

Dull colours that drain energy from adjacent vivid colours.

Primary colours

Colours that cannot result from a mix of other colours, but from which all other colours can be mixed.

Process colour

Colours produced from the mixture of CMYK print separations rather than a single plate.

Projected colour

Colours that project themselves beyond their boundaries to tint larger neutral areas with their own hue.

RGB

Red, green, and blue, the three primary colours used in transmitted colour to produce all other displayable colours.

Ruling colour
The colour positioned in the middle of a group of analogous colours.

Saturation
The purity and brightness of a colour.

Secondary colours
The result of mixing primary colours two at a time in equal amounts.

Shade
The result of adding black to a hue.

Simultaneous contrast
Apparent changes in hue, value, and/or chroma that are created by the after-image of adjacent colours.

Spot colour
A custom pre-mixed ink printed from its own plate rather than produced by the process colours.

Subtractive colour
Colours reflected by pigment that become darker in value when mixed with additional colours.

Tertiary colours
The result of mixing a primary and a secondary colour in equai amounts.

Tint
The result of adding white to a hue.

Triads
Three hues equidistance from each other on the colour wheel.

Vanishing boundaries
When boundaries between tightly juxtaposed shapes become unrecognisable due to selection of analogous colour or equal value.

Vector-based programs
Computer programs that use vector images, images that are defined mathematically as a series of points joined by lines that are resolution-independent.

Vibrating boundaries
The sensation of movement produced when areas of contrasting colour are tightly juxtaposed.

Wavelength
The distance between successive peaks of the electromagnetic waves of light that determines both visibility of light and colour.

Subjective Colour Selection

advance
    spatial 27–9
    warm–cool 30–1
after-image 14–15, 16, 21
analogous colours 38
area 32–5

boundaries 27, 36, 38–9, 43, 58
brightness 36
brilliance 43

chroma 16, 21–3, 31, 34–5, 43
colour schemes 11
colour wheel 55–6
complementary hues 14, 16, 21
contrast 27, 38, 62
    simultaneous 16–23, 59–60

depth 26–33, 63–4
distance
    optical mixture 44
    size 32–3
    spatial advance/recession 27–9
    warm–cool 30–1

greys 16, 40–1, 61–2

hard boundaries 27, 38, 43
harmony 38

large areas 32–5
limited palettes 54
luminosity 21

mixing 56

neutral colours 16, 40–1, 61–2
neutralisation 16, 21

optical mixture 44–5, 53–4

palette limitations 54
parasites 40–1
patterns 38–41, 44–5
poster cards 51–64
primary colours 56
projected colour 42–3, 57–8

radiance 21
recession
    spatial 27–9
    warm–cool 30–1
repetitive patterns 38–41, 44–5

saturation 38
secondary colours 56
simultaneous contrast 16–23, 59–60
size
    chroma 34–5
    colour 36–7
    distance 32–3
small areas 32–5
soft boundaries 27, 38, 43
spatial advance/recession 27–9
successive contrasts *see* after-image

temperature 30–1
tertiary colours 56
tints 14

value 14, 16, 20, 27, 38, 43
vanishing boundaries 38–9
vibrating boundaries 38–9
vivid colours 40–1

warm–cool distance 30–1

RECOMMENDED READING

Albers, Josef. (1963). *Interaction of Color*
Massachusetts: The Murray Printing Co.

Carter, Rob. (2002). *Digital Color and Type*
East Sussex: RotoVision Books

Cohen, Sandee. (1998). *Freehand 8 for Windows and Macintosh*
California: Peachpit Press

Favre, Jean-Paul. November, Andre. (1973). *Color and Communication*
Zurich: ABC Editions

Itten, Johannes. (2001). *The Elements of Color*
Weinheim: John Wiley and Sons, Inc.

Livingston, Isabella and Alan. (1998). *Dictionary of Graphic Design and Designers*
London: Thames and Hudson

Luckiesh, M. (1965). *Visual Illusions – Their Causes, Characteristics, and Applications*
Toronto: Dover Publications, Inc.

Lumgair, Christopher. (1999). *Teach Yourself Illustrator 8.0 for Macintosh and Windows*
London: Hodder Headline Plc.

Page, Hilary. (1994). *Colour Right from the Start*
New York: Watson-Guptill Publications

Pipes, Alan. (2001). *Production for Graphic Designers: Third Edition*
London: Laurence King Publishing

Powell, William, F. (1984). *Color and How to Use It*
California: Walter Foster Publishing, Inc.

Stockton, James. (1984). *Designer's Guide to Color*
San Francisco: Chronicle Books

Wong, Wucius. (1987). *Principles of Color Design*
New York: Van Nostrand Reinhold

Zelanski, Paul. Fisher, Mary P. (1989). *Colour*
London: The Herbert Press Limited

ACKNOWLEDGEMENTS

I would like to acknowledge the following people for helping
make this book possible:

Roger Gould, Phil Jones, Kirsten Hardie, Martin Coyne and
all the staff at AIB. Peter Fiell, Ian Noble and Al Murphy as
without their generous encouragement and advice this would
just be an old file on my computer. Brian Morris,
Natalia Price-Cabrera and Eloyse Tan Chiew Lan at AVA
Publishing SA for their vision and months of continuous help.
Tom Rothwell, James Hoxley and the team at Explosive for
their support and guidance. Paul and Clare, Jon Darke,
Brad Le Riche, David Tryhorn, Christopher Parkinson,
and especially Sam Smith for their enthusiasm and support.
Special thanks to Aurora Aspen whose love and
understanding has been an inspiration from the
outset of this project.

Most of all thanks to my parents for everything above,
and much more.

In memory of Ivy Violet Bellamy. Grandma and friend.